ANIMALS
IN THE
FIRST WORLD WAR

Neil R. Storey

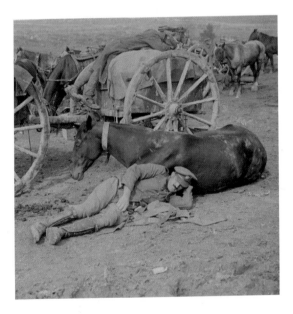

SHIRE PUBLICATIONS

Published in Great Britain in 2014 by Shire Publications Ltd, PO Box 883, Oxford, OX1 9PL, UK.

PO Box 3985, New York, NY 10185-3985, USA.

E-mail: shire@shirebooks.co.uk   www.shirebooks.co.uk

A CIP catalogue record for this book is available from the British Library.

Shire Library no. 790.   ISBN-13: 978 0 74781 367 5

Neil R. Storey has asserted his right under the Copyright, Designs and Patents Act, 1988, to be identified as the author of this book.

Designed by Tony Truscott Designs, Sussex, UK and typeset in Perpetua and Gill Sans.

Cover design by Peter Ashley (image from author's collection). Back cover: German gas mask for a dog, courtesy of Australian War Memorial.

Printed in China through Worldprint Ltd.

14 15 16 17 18   10 9 8 7 6 5 4 3 2 1

TITLE PAGE IMAGE
Soldier of the transport section of the Devon Regiment and his horse share a moment's rest amid the turmoil of war, near Fricourt, 7 August 1916.

CONTENTS PAGE IMAGE
Territorial Force Royal Field Artillerymen, horses in harness to gun and limber at Forest Gate, London 1914.

ACKNOWLEDGEMENTS
Images are acknowledged as follows:

Art Gallery of New South Wales, Sydney, Australia / The Bridgeman Art Library, page 8; Imperial War Museum, title page and pages 11, 20 (bottom), 24, 30 (both), 31 (top), 33 (bottom left), 37, 38 (bottom), 39 (bottom), 40 (bottom left), 44 (both), 45, 50 (top), 51; Library of Congress, pages 29 and 41; Mary Evans Picture Library, page 42; National Army Museum, page 7; Steve Reed, pages 52–3.

All other images are from the author's collection.

CONTENTS

INTRODUCTION

A NIMALS have been involved in warfare as long as man could ride a horse into battle or train a dog to attack. Early recorded history has horses in action carrying mounted troops and towing chariots in ancient Egypt, Greece and Rome. Even in this early period the warhorse became iconic in statues, jewellery, coins and mosaics, and was eulogised in script. One of the earliest recorded animals distinguished for its long, brave and noble performance both on campaign and in battle was Bucephalus, the warhorse of Alexander the Great, which, despite being mortally wounded, carried his master out of the fray unscathed at the Battle of Hydaspes in 326 BC. Alexander ensured his loyal horse was buried with full military honours and was even depicted on coins. Empire-building saw troops move over thousands of miles; most enduring is the true story of how Hannibal fought and crossed the Alps with elephants and 4,000 horsemen during the Second Punic War in 218 BC. In Britannia the Iceni tribe of East Anglia also venerated their horses in the early decades of the new millennium; they were depicted on their coinage and were led in battle against the Romans by Queen Boudicca in her horse-drawn chariot in AD 60. Indeed, for the majority of the next 1,000 years, campaigns, crusades, battles and wars were conducted on horseback – from the mounted cavalry of William the Conqueror in 1066 to Cromwell's 'Ironsides' with their 'lobster-tailed' helmets and Prince Rupert's cavalry during the English Civil War (1642–51).

Warfare changed after the defeat of Napoleon at Waterloo in 1815. No longer was Britain embroiled in a costly European war, and the Industrial Revolution enabled the development and mass production of better firearms and weaponry. Britain became wealthy and powerful as it explored the world for gold, diamonds, minerals and resources, laying claim to them in the name of the Queen. Despite all this modernisation, steam trains and wheeled vehicles were still not practical modes of transport for soldiers wanting to cross rugged and uncharted terrain; it still fell to horses, ponies and mules to carry burdens, pull the supply wagons and bravely carry the cavalrymen into action as Britain fought its 'small wars' to acquire, occupy and defend the Empire.

Opposite:
The well-travelled
ship's cat of HMS
Renown, 1906.

Sadly, although soldiers would care for their mounts – for often their lives depended upon them – military horses were, in general, treated very much as a means to an end until the latter part of the nineteenth century. At this point, public concern for those less fortunate – be they human or animal – was seen as a worthy, Christian and benevolent attitude, particularly amongst those who had benefited from the 1870 Education Act, in which the focus was not only the 'three Rs' but also the importance of national pride and duty to God, Queen and country.

When the British Empire was at its military apogee the works of artists such as Lady Butler (Elizabeth Southerden Thompson) and Richard Caton Woodville evocatively captured the notable battles and engagement of the British Army. New technological developments meant that prints of their works were affordable to far greater numbers than ever before, and the homes of the patriotic and sentimental Victorians could not be without a Butler or Woodville for their wall. Prints and line illustrations of such actions or deeds of derring-do appeared in all manner of magazines, periodicals and books as visuals to inspire patriotic fervour and pride in the British Empire.

One of the first images to capture the public's imagination in this genre was Lady Butler's *Remnants of an Army*, depicting William Brydon, an assistant surgeon in the Bengal Army, on his horse. Both are clearly battle-worn and desperately exhausted as they approach the gates of Jalalabad, for they were the first of but a few stragglers to make it back out of 16,000 soldiers and camp followers from the retreat from Kabul in 1842 during the First Afghan War. Painted during the Second Afghan War, *Remnants of an Army* was both poignant and topical when it was first exhibited at the Royal Academy summer exhibition in 1879.

Although prints of *Remnants of an Army* sold well, it did not show the glory so many Victorians wanted to see associated with the gallant actions of the British Army; thus it was to the preceding great victory of the British Army that Lady Butler turned in 1881. *Scotland Forever* depicts the charge of the Scots Greys at the Battle of Waterloo – just as it commenced and the war cry 'Scotland Forever' was on the lips of their commander. All the men look magnificent in their black bearskin cap and scarlet tunics in full cry with swords aloft, but it is the heavy grey mounts, so vividly captured and expressively detailed, which dominate the picture. The painting was enormously popular but, like so many Victorian images, it did not show the cost in life and limb: the charge ended with 200 men and 224 horses killed or wounded.

The theme of horses dramatically conveying the drama of the actions in their expressions is repeated again and again in some of the most popular battle pictures of the late-Victorian era, such as Caton Woodville's *Saving the Guns at Maiwand* (1883), his *Charge of the Light Brigade* (1894), and numerous

renditions by various artists of the last full cavalry charge of the British Army by the 21st Lancers at the Battle of Omdurman on 2 September 1898.

Popular paintings and books reflected the new sentimentality and awareness of the plight of animals beloved of the Victorians, epitomised in such books as *Black Beauty* by Anna Sewell (1877) and Marshall Saunder's best-selling *Beautiful Joe: A Dog's Own Story* (1893). Charities, in their appeals for donations published in newspapers, in magazines or on posters, often illustrated them with images of attractive young girls with imploring eyes, or animals (especially dogs) shown in similar demeanour. It was not long before a variety of animals began to join the high-profile military horse – indeed a number of regiments already had their own mascots that would feature in formal parades – but the animals that appealed most to Victorian audiences were those that demonstrated selfless loyalty, good practical work and bravery of their own accord.

One of the first to capture the hearts of the British populace was Dick, a fox terrier, who remained by the side of Surgeon Reynolds during the attack of the Zulu impis at Rorke's Drift on 22 January 1879. In truth he did depart once, to dash at one of the Zulu warriors who ventured over the defences and sent him back with a nip in his shin! Dick appears, standing loyally beside his master in the thick of the action, in the 1880 painting *The Defence of Rorke's Drift* by Alphonse de Neuville. Then there was Jock of the Black Watch who joined the regiment at Edinburgh Castle in 1882, proceeded with them

The Charge of the Light Brigade took place on 25 October 1854 and was immortalised by poets and artists – this painting is by Richard Caton Woodville, 1894.

The Defence of Rorke's Drift (1879) by Alphonse de Neuville. Note Dick the fox terrier in the midst of the fray near Surgeon Reynolds.

to campaign service in Egypt, was wounded at El Teb and Kirbehan in 1885, recovered and eventually died of old age while still with his beloved regiment in 1891.

During the South African War (1899–1902) there was a plethora of pets: the feisty Irish terrier 'Scout' of the 1st Royal Dragoons, who took part in the storming of the Tugela Heights and led the way over Pieter's Hill; Jemima the hen, who helped keep the Royals fed at Ladysmith; and Modder the loyal pet dog of the 3rd Grenadier Guards whose postcard image sold by the thousand.

And who could fail to be moved by the story of Jennie, the loyal old Drum Horse of the 7th Dragoon Guards, the only one to survive of the black horses on which the regiment was mounted at the commencement of the South African War. After the campaign every officer, NCO and man in the regiment was so proud of her that the Commanding Officer obtained permission to purchase her from the Government out of regimental funds; she was returned to England and became the regimental pet. Jennie died in 1905 from enteritis, caused by the sand that had got into her system during the war. Jennie was indeed fortunate to make it back. Out of the 520,000 remounts supplied for the British Army during the South African War some 326,073 of them died, most of them through disease or exhaustion rather than fire from the enemy.

The Royal Society for the Prevention of Cruelty to Animals (RSPCA), which had been founded as The Society for the Prevention of Cruelty to Animals (SPCA) back in 1824, had already voiced its concerns over the treatment of horses during the Franco-Prussian War (1870–71). The military had run a small Army Veterinary Service since 1796 but it was only in 1880 that the Army Veterinary Department was formed, with its own specialist Army Veterinary School established at Aldershot the same year. With the publication of high-profile images and stories of horses and animals in war and in response to a ground swell of public sympathy, another organisation sprung up: 'Our Dumb Friends League' (ODFL) was founded in 1897 'to encourage in individuals humanity to dumb animals by education, co-operation and, where desirable, grants of money.' They knew that sometimes it was the little things that could mean the difference between life and death for a pet dog. The families of Reservists called to serve in the South African War often struggled to pay the fee for a dog licence while their main

Below left: Modder, the mascot of 3rd Battalion, Grenadier Guards, resplendent with Queen's South Africa and King's South Africa medals at the collar.

Below right: Bronco, a juvenile baboon, who was regimental pet of 2nd Battalion, the Norfolk Regiment, c. 1905.

breadwinner was away, so the ODFL organised a fund for this, saving many healthy pets from being put down unnecessarily. The RSPCA also campaigned during the South African War for a properly trained corps to put down all seriously wounded animals humanely during the conflict. This was not enacted during the war but did lead directly to the new, enlarged and improved Army Veterinary Corps (AVC) in 1903.

At a National Peace Congress held in London in May 1912 the concerns about the treatment and welfare of animals in war were raised anew. A resolution was adopted requesting an extension of the provisions of the Geneva Convention to wounded horses and other animals employed in warfare. In that same year ODFL began its Blue Cross Fund specifically for the relief of animals affected by war. During the Balkan War the RSPCA sent £1,175 to Lady Lowther, wife of the British Ambassador at the British Embassy in Constantinople. With this money an SPCA was started there which cared for 150 horses at the front; buffaloes, oxen and donkeys were fed for five months; and 13,500 weekly rations for animals were distributed. In March 1913 the newly created ODFL Blue Cross fund sent £500 for the relief of suffering horses returning from the Balkan War. In 1913, RSPCA Council member Sir George Greenwood, liberal MP for Peterborough, raised the question again of whether the Geneva Convention could be widened to protect veterinary surgeons. He was assured that 'it would be borne in mind' by the delegates at the next peace conference ... but the following year was 1914.

As the First World War approached the scene was set for the greatest challenges ever to face animals in the history of warfare and the unprecedented public interest in the deeds and welfare of animals in that war was assured.

ODFL Blue Cross Fund appeal poster, 1917. (IWM PST 6189)

Opposite:
A fine study of a trooper in the Berkshire Yeomanry by R. Caton Woodville, c. 1910.

MASCOTS AND PETS

O VER THE YEARS before and throughout the First World War a veritable menagerie of mascots or pets could be found across the regiments and corps of the British Army, and aboard many ships of the Royal Navy. With the creation of the Royal Flying Corps and Royal Naval Air Service (RNAS) they soon acquired and adopted their mascots too, and all manner of animals were used on the Home Front for patriotic purposes and at fundraising events throughout the war.

Historically the ships of the Royal Navy have carried a variety of animals on their decks and in their holds: cows and goats to provide fresh milk; chickens or ducks for fresh eggs; and pigs to slaughter for fresh meat on long journeys, even during the First World War. One such creature was a pig that was spotted swimming in the water after the German light cruiser *Dresden* was sunk by the Royal Navy on 14 May 1915. A sailor from HMS *Glasgow*, despite nearly being drowned by the frightened pig, succeeded in rescuing her. Despite her gender, she was still given the name Tirpitz (after the Imperial German Admiral Alfred von Tirpitz). She became HMS *Glasgow*'s mascot for a year and was then transferred to Whale Island Gunnery School, Portsmouth in 1916. Unfortunately Tirpitz made a nuisance of herself and was returned to Captain John Luce (former commander of HMS *Glasgow* and now the commander of the RNAS Training Establishment at Cranwell in Lincolnshire), who soon saw to it that Tirpitz was sold at a charity auction in aid of the British Red Cross in December 1917 where she raised some 400 guineas. The head of Tirpitz was mounted at the expense of her final owner, the Duke of Portland, and presented to the Imperial War Museum; the Duke also had two of her trotters turned into the handles of a carving set.

Sailors were also known to return from exotic climes with outlandish pets such as monkeys or brightly coloured parrots, and many a captain had brought his own dog along for the journey or acquired one along the way. Indeed, the crew of HMS *Centurion* brought back a dog, a goose and a rabbit (which they named Pip, Squeak and Wilfred after popular cartoon characters

Opposite:
Lieutenant Harry Colebourn of the Canadian Royal Army Veterinary Corps with his female black bear cub, which would become the inspiration for *Winnie the Pooh*.

'Pelerous Jack' of the Royal Navy battle cruiser HMS *New Zealand*.

The dog, a goose and a rabbit (named after Pip, Squeak and Wilfred, popular cartoon characters in the *Daily Mirror*) and a donkey are taken on board HMS *Centurion* as refugees from Gallipoli during service in the Black Sea in 1918–19.

in the *Daily Mirror*) and a donkey they rescued and took on board as refugees from Gallipoli during service in the Black Sea in 1918–19.

Sturdy and tenacious fighting dogs such as bulldogs and Staffordshire bull terriers such as 'Pelerous Jack' of the Royal Navy battle cruiser HMS *New Zealand* made good subjects for patriotic postcards, in books or magazines. Jack joined the ship in 1913, was present at the Battle of Jutland,

and achieved the rank of Leading Sea Dog before his discharge in October 1919 when he was presented to the City of Auckland, together with his silver collar, a gift from the New Zealanders of Transvaal. There were also the likes of loyal old Shanks, the dog mascot of HMS *Patia* who was seventeen years old in 1914 and by that time had spent fourteen years of his life at sea during which time he crossed the Pacific and the Mediterranean, going as far afield as China and Egypt, gaining over 160,000 miles at sea to his credit.

The earliest mascots or pets in the Royal Navy were cats, which were kept on ships to tackle the rats and mice on board. This was a valuable job on a long journey when the crew depended on the preservation of their stored food from the greedy feeding of rodents. If the cat did a good job it would soon be loved and cherished by the grateful crew, a feline friend to be stroked and played with during moments of rest outside the hard-working hours on a man-of-war. But that was not all: ancient tradition among mariners firmly believed that cats were lucky creatures to have aboard ships, and that cats were endowed with magic powers to protect ships from dangerous weather. Many sailors held the belief that if the ship's cat sneezed it meant rain, if it licked its fur against the grain a hailstorm was coming, and if it was frisky they could expect wind. It is interesting to note there is more than a grain of truth in these old superstitions, for modern science has proved cats can indeed detect changes in the weather because their sensitive inner ears are affected by low atmospheric pressure, a common precursor of stormy weather, which causes nervousness or restless behaviour in cats.

Most battleships of the navies of the main belligerents during the First World War had a ship's cat. In the Royal Navy they were often photographed in the barrel of one

A Christmas greetings card featuring the ship's cat of HMS *Topaze*, 1915.

15

of the ship's big guns or in the middle of a life preserver ring bearing the ship's name, as greetings cards for the men serving on board. Examples include the beautiful short-coated black cats Smut of HMS *Superb* and Side Boy of HMS *Neptune*, whose images went on to appear on many of the popular 'lucky black cat' postcards of the day; and lucky they were, for both battleships saw action at the Battle of Jutland on 31 May 1916 and both cats and battleships survived the war. Then there was Hoskyn, the ship's cat of HMS *Chester* who steadfastly carried on during Jutland (the captain's sheepdog was wounded in the same action). Less fortunate was Jimmy, the long-haired tortoiseshell who had been adopted from a wounded Australian soldier by a ship's cook aboard HMS *King George V*. Jimmy was also present at Jutland but suffered a shrapnel wound to his left ear when a shell exploded near him on deck. Jimmy was transferred to HMS *Renown* in 1916 and finally retired to a Chelsea cats' home in London where he died in 1924. Other cats were lost when their ships went down, such as Lyddite, the mascot of the destroyer HMS *Shark*, sunk with the loss of many of her crew at Jutland, and Togo, who had been on board the battleship HMS *Irresistible* for years before the First World War and went with the battleship to the Dardanelles where the *Irresistible* struck a mine and sank off the Turkish coast on 18 March 1915.

The band and regimental mascot and pets of the Welsh Regiment, c. 1914.

Despite a heroic attempt to save Togo by Leading Stoker William Burrows, tragically both were drowned. Cats carried on doing valuable work through war and peace until the Royal Navy banned them in 1975 from all ships on the ocean, along with all other pet animals, citing grounds of hygiene.

Regimental mascots are recorded in the British Army as far back as the eighteenth century, one of the earliest of them being a goat the Royal Welsh Fusiliers had with them during the American War of Independence (1775–83). Regimental mascots were used for ceremonial occasions to represent the locality from which the regiment was recruited, regimental tradition or the campaigns in which the regiment had fought, rather than having a specific purpose or use by the unit. By the late nineteenth century there was a bewildering array of regimental mascots, from sheep, goats, dogs, birds, antelopes and donkeys to baboons, apes, bears and deer; each one was given a smart soldier, often a drummer, to look after them, feed them, ensure they were well groomed and handled well on parade (in some cases, such as a headstrong ram, two handlers might be employed), when they would often be marched alongside the Drum Major. In fact, many regiments even had their own titles for the soldiers charged with this duty; for example in the Welsh Regiment the handlers of the mascot were styled 'Goat Majors', while in the case of the Royal Warwickshire Regiment the two drummers in charge of their antelope were known as the 'Buck Leader' and 'Assistant Buck Leader'.

Every mascot would be kitted out with some fine coat, saddlecloth or harness bearing a suitable regimental device, a form of adapted uniform, or decorative medallions or precious metal fittings presented by officers, nobility, members of the Royal Family or even the monarch. They were also governed by a set of rules, as explained by Major T. J. Edwards in *Mascots and Pets of the Services* (1953):

> Regimental Mascots are not official, by which term is meant that War Office authority is not given, nor is it required, for their adoption. They are sometimes given 'Regimental Numbers', names and ranks by units for identification purposes, but that is purely a regimental matter. Sometimes, also, they are fed from Government stocks when civilian sources are found to be inadequate, but only on repayment.

Some mascots can even be seen wearing medals upon their collar or coat from the campaigns where they and their regiment were present; these would not have been issued to any mascot or regimental pet but bought out of regimental funds instead. The only official medal to be directly awarded to animals for gallantry or devotion to duty is the PDSA Dickin Medal, instituted in 1943.

Although there would be no official medals for them, many regimental mascots did proceed to war stations and active service abroad with their respective regiments, and occasionally new ones were presented or acquired along the way. Some of the mascots that went to war were Leitrim Boy, the Irish wolfhound mascot of the Irish Guards, and Jack, the old black labrador

The bulldog
mascot of
5th Battalion,
the Royal Scots,
c. 1914.

of the Royal Dublin Fusiliers. Poor Taffy IV, the goat of 2nd Battalion, Welsh Regiment, died in Béthune, France on 20 January 1915. Dear little Jean, the loyal dog o Captain R. Macfarlane of 2nd Battalion, the Black Watch, had accompanied her master abroad to serve in the Middle East until he was killed in action at Istabulat on 21 April 1917. She was then adopted as the regimental pet of the 2nd Battalion and stayed with them through the rest of the war. There was even a pig: Muriel was found in a jungle near Sialkot, India, and was adopted by members of 1st Battalion, the Royal Inniskilling Fusiliers in 1919.

For the most dramatic acquisition during the war, however, General Sir Tom Bridges, Commander of the 19th Division, takes some beating. When he was on leave in Paris during the spring of 1916 he spotted what turned out to be a young lion, which the owner had won in a Red Cross raffle a few days earlier! Bridges was offered the lion and he took it back to his headquarters in a champagne hamper. 'Poilu' became the mascot of the 19th Division, was put in the care of Bombardier Leather and was allowed to roam free around the grounds of HQ, becoming very popular among the men on his trips up to the trenches. He grew very quickly, however, and after rumblings from the Adjutant-General and the C-in-C expressing displeasure at 'carnivorous mascots', Poilu was sent to England, where he spent the rest of his life in a private zoo until his death in June 1935.

Mascots were not just a British phenomenon: commonwealth troops had their own too. Numerous Australian regiments took an eclectic mix of dogs, wallabies and their kangaroo mascots with them to Egypt before proceeding to Gallipoli and left a number of them in Cairo Zoo. In 1916 there were so many wallabies brought over to England by Australians on their way to the Western Front they had their own 'paddock' in Portsmouth. Floss, a

Little billy goat mascot of the Sherwood Rangers, 1914.

Peter, the St Bernard mascot of 2nd Battalion, Honourable Artillery Company, 1916.

bitch fox terrier from Sir Walter Long's kennels at Trowbridge, had been given to Driver 'Ike' Lowndes who taught her a number of tricks – she could pray, play a piano, sit at a table and give orders to a waiter and even jump a skipping rope.

Floss became the mascot of the New Zealand Army Rugby Football Team when they toured Britain in 1917.

While still over in Canada, English-born Lieutenant Harry Colebourn of the Canadian Royal Army Veterinary Corps bought a female black bear cub from a hunter for $20 in White River, Ontario, Canada, while en route

Nancy, the springbok mascot of the 4th South African Regiment, at Delville Wood, Somme, France, in February 1918. (IWM Q_010675)

to England. He named it 'Winnie' after his adopted hometown of Winnipeg, Manitoba, and brought it with him where she became mascot for the Fort Garry Horse while they were on Salisbury Plain. When Colebourn and the Fort Garry Horse proceeded to France he left Winnie in the care of London Zoo and officially donated her after the war. Thousands of visitors came to see the little bear, and children loved her, among them a certain Christopher Robin Milne who named his toy bear after her. When young Christopher Robin's father, Mr A. A. Milne, came to write his now world-famous and enduring book, it was to his son's bear he turned for a name for its central character – Winnie the Pooh.

Mascots that remained at home often made appearances at recruiting parades and wartime fundraising events. The Notts and Derby's ram, Derby XII, which had been presented by the Duke of Devonshire in 1912, was just one of them. He made countless appearances and must have marched hundreds of miles over those years; his duty done, Derby the ram passed away in July 1919. Other mascots were found along the way, even while soldiers were on home service. For example, the Sherwood Rangers Yeomanry had a fine young billy goat with them as their mascot while on coastal defence duties in Norfolk during the opening months of the war, as did the Montgomeryshire Yeomanry. As the war progressed, generous benefactors would often be keen to present a fine animal to the new army battalions, such as Mr J. S. Hall of Langdon Hill in Essex who, in 1916, presented Tiger, a pedigree light brindle Great Dane, to the new Royal Fusiliers battalion raised in his district in 1916. Among the most unusual anywhere in Britain was the pair of baby orang-utans adopted by the Warwickshire Yeomanry in 1915.

It should also be remembered that there were many furry and feathered mascots who helped to raise thousands of pounds for war charities. Some dogs became well-known presences, such as Bob at Liverpool, Prince at Crewe, Cymro at Rhyl and many others, notably Brum, a brown spaniel-retriever mongrel who had the monopoly at Euston Station. He would trot up and down the station with his collecting box on his back, barking to attract attention and raising a paw to say thank-you when a donation was dropped in his box.

Nancy the St Bernard, doing 'her bit' for the British Red Cross Society.

Outstanding among the breeds of dogs raising money for the British Red Cross Society was the St Bernard. A naturally kind and impressive canine, the St Bernard was already established in the minds of the British public as a selfless, caring animal, as it featured in paintings and stories that often told of rescues of people buried, injured or trapped by snow in the breed's native Switzerland. The dogs were soon appearing at events, often wearing a collecting box to help raise money for wounded soldiers.

Among the feathered mascots adopted at home was a fledgling crow that fell from its nest and was nursed back to health by the wounded soldiers who adopted it as their mascot at Sheffield Base Hospital in 1916. The singular efforts of Mr Fyson of Warboys, Hertfordshire and his 'VC Cockerel' should also be recorded. The cockerel was entered into British Farmers' Red Cross Fund sales across the country as a novel way to encourage donations. The bird would be bid on even though people knew that Mr Warboys would actually keep him, and the money would go to the fund. The cockerel regularly realised over £70 in the sales and had raised almost £8,000 by the spring of 1918.

Mr Fyson of Warboys, Hertfordshire and his 'VC Cockerel'.

Total amount to Apr 16ᵗʰ 1918. £7863.

Fyson with his V.C. Cockerel at Spalding, Aug. 6. 1917

Amount raised £330, making a total of £5,080 for the Red +. With Cup presented by Mr H. Brown,

Organiser of the British Farmers' Red Cross Fund

Most of the regimental mascots were fortunate enough to make it through the war years on the home front, but sadly a few of them passed away or were killed in accidents before the end of hostilities. Each of them would usually be given some form of honours funeral as a mark of affection and appreciation for the animal's faithful service. A coffin would be made (most pitiful would be the small boxes for good ratter cats and small dogs), borne to the graveside by smartly turned-out pall bearers. Troops would parade; the coffin would be lowered on streamers into its tiny grave, the last post sounded and shots fired in salute, but the padre would not have read a formal service. Among the losses were Tommy Brown, mascot of the Motor Transport Section, 3rd Division Supply Column of the Australian Field Force; he had been the only koala brought alive by the force to England. When in July 1916 Billy the bulldog, regimental pet of the Royal Inniskilling Fusiliers, died in Dawlish, South Devon, he was given an honours funeral, a stone was erected on his grave inscribed with his name and regiment, and his death was even reported in *The Times* newspaper. But for an ongoing legacy from a mascot that did not make it all the way through there is Freda, the Harlequin Great Dane mascot of the New Zealand Rifle Brigade when they were stationed at Cannock Chase, Staffordshire. When she died in 1918 her human comrades erected a headstone, which has been renewed and maintained by the local community and Friends of Cannock Chase ever since. Today, working dogs and their owners are encouraged to attend the service at Freda's grave on Armistice Day to celebrate the loyalty and service of such dogs.

The funeral of a much-loved Royal Naval Air Service mascot cat, c. 1915.

23

G. R.

WANTED

MEN FOR THE

ARMY REMOUNT DEPT.

FOR DURATION OF WAR.

AGE 25 TO 40

PAY: 1s. 5d. to 1s. 8d. A DAY, EVERYTHING FOUND
(while Serving in England).

3s. A DAY, EVERYTHING FOUND
(while Serving Overseas).

Separation Allowances at Usual Army Rates.

ONLY MEN THOROUGHLY ACCUSTOMED TO HORSES REQUIRED.

APPLY:

GOD SAVE THE KING.

41M. W 72—550. 3/15. G.15. 376.   Printed by Hazell, Watson & Viney, Ld., 52, Long Acre, W.C.

HORSES AT WAR

W HEN THE First World War broke out in August 1914 the entire British Army had just eighty motor vehicles. All other transportation of guns, munitions, men, equipment, supplies and fuel relied on horse-power, and with the mobilisation and the expansion of the army, horses would be required in unprecedented numbers. An immediate call for an additional 25,000 was made in the first six months of the war – it soon became apparent that five times that number would actually be required. The sole responsibility for this massive task fell to the Army Remounts Service, and a National Emergency Impressment Order was issued under Section 115 of the Army Act whereby locally appointed purchasing officers were empowered to impress horses, vehicles and equipment for the war effort. Soon market places and village greens were filling up with lines of horses, piles of tack and commandeered carts from farms and businesses in the locality as local yeomanry units and territorials were allotted their mounts watched by large crowds of curious onlookers. Regular cavalry units already had their own tried and trusted horses and were seen trotting out of their barracks, down to their nearest railway station and loading their horses onto cattle wagons, then off to Dover and the crossing to France. The British Expeditionary Force proceeded to France with 40,000 horses and mules. Each one of them had to be hoisted aboard and into the holds of the ships; despite the best efforts of the AVC officers and men, for some horses the trauma of this unfamiliar experience caused fatal heart attacks, and some went berserk in the fetid and cramped conditions during the crossing.

As the opening weeks and months of the war passed, both regular and territorial units needed fresh supplies of horses for new recruits and to replace those wounded or killed in action. The experienced horsemen would comment that although the horses that were supplied were of good quality, fit and healthy, many had not had a rider on their back before and did not understand the spurs commands – riders soon learned that if they wanted to get the horse to move, the order had to be given verbally.

Opposite:
Army Remount
Department
poster, 1915.
(IWM PST 7678)

A fine study of
a trooper of
the Derbyshire
Yeomanry and
his mount, 1915.

Requisitioned
horses and carts in
the market place
at East Dereham,
Norfolk in 1914.

Left: Farriers of the Norfolk Regiment shoeing one of the battalion transport horses at their field forge 'somewhere in England', c. 1915.

Middle: Brass trade badges denoted the trade proficiencies. From left to right: 'wheeler' badge for a wheelwright or carpenter; saddler or harness maker; and farrier.

Below: An anaesthetised horse of the Derbyshire Yeomanry receives treatment from a local vet while on home service in 1915.

Above: Royal Horse Artillery watering their horses at the trough. Note the riding instructor in the foreground and even the mascot dog posing for the photo, c. 1914.

In action, horses pulled artillery guns and limbers, supply trucks and ambulance wagons, sometimes belly-deep in mud — whole gun teams could be lost in the liquefied mire of the shell-holed landscape or wiped out by the drop of a shell.

Horses were in action from the opening exchanges of gunfire in 1914 right through to the bitter end. First was an engagement at Néry, France, on 1 September 1914 when all members of L Battery, Royal Horse Artillery were either killed or wounded; Captain Bradbury, Sergeant Major Dorrell and Sergeant Nelson continued to fire their field gun to hold back the enemy.

Right: The official British Military Cavalry Training Manual, still being reprinted, with amendments in 1915.

Opposite: Artillery gun and limber with horses charging into action was a popular image on recruiting posters and adverts during the early war years.

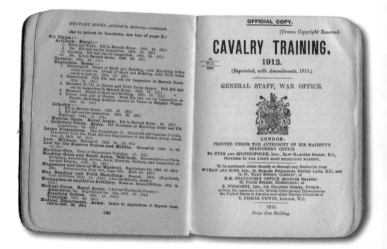

AT THE FRONT!

Every fit Briton
should join our brave men
at the Front.

ENLIST NOW.

Right: Mules carrying shells struggle through the mud near Ypres on the Western Front, c. 1917. (IWM Q_005941)

Below: Horses struggle through the mud and battle-scarred landscape to pull the limber taking ammunition forward to guns along the Lesboeufs Road, outside Flers on the Somme, France, November 1916. (IWM Q2980)

Opposite, top: German transport driver and horse team on the Western Front wearing gas masks, 1917. (IWM Q_050651)

Other cavalry charges included the XII Royal Lancers (Prince of Wales') successful charge against the Germans at the Battle of Moy on 28 August 1914 and the legendary charge of the 4th and 12th Australian Light Horse Regiments during the Battle of Beersheba (Third Battle of Gaza, 31 October 1917), when they captured the last remaining Ottoman trenches defending Beersheba and continued their charge into the town and captured the garrison. The last cavalry charge of the First World War was the charge of

the 7th Dragoon Guards to capture the Lessines and the Dender crossings in Belgium as the clocks were striking 11 o'clock to mark the end of hostilities. In *The Horse in War* J. M. Brereton wrote in tribute:

> On campaign, riding and reading the horse for months on end, sleeping in the open only a few yards behind the picket lines at night, and suffering the same privations, the soldier came to regard his horse as almost an extension of his entire being.

Top: Cap badge of the Army Veterinary Corps during the First World War.

Out of the 256,000 horses lost by British forces on the Western Front, fewer than 58,000 were killed by enemy fire. The biggest killer of horses in 1914 was death from overexposure; disease and sickness would also take their toll over the ensuing years. When poison gas attacks began in 1915 gas masks had to be hastily devised for both men and animals. Men would bind a pad soaked in urine over their mouths and nostrils; horses would have nose plugs put up their nostrils, held in place with safety pins. Improved gas masks were developed throughout the war whereby a large canvas and flannel bag would be attached to the

Above: A rare RSPCA Sick and Wounded Horses Fund badge, worn by the auxiliaries the charity provided for the Army Veterinary Corps.

This postcard, though sentimental to modern eyes, reflects the close bond between soldiers and their horses living and working together at war.

Comrades.

31

horse's head with straps. The horse would often assume this was a nosebag and could chew through it in about three minutes as it rootled around for non-existent fodder within it.

Thoroughbred horses were particularly prone to shell-shock: some would suddenly give under their riders, sweat profusely or refuse to go on. Injured horses came under the care of the Army Veterinary Corps. Every cavalry and infantry brigade had a veterinary officer who would often work in extremely dangerous conditions providing emergency aid to horses near the front line and if necessary, organised the sending of serious cases to field or base hospitals; if a horse could not walk it would be transported to hospital by specially built ambulance.

Both the Blue Cross and RSPCA worked indefatigably for animal welfare in every theatre of war. When war broke out the RSPCA offered its services to the War Office but was initially rebuffed because the authorities were convinced the provisions already established in the AVC were adequate and no outside assistance was required. Undaunted, the RSPCA appealed to its own inspectors to join the AVC. Ninety of them answered the call. The knowledge and experience of the RSPCA workers proved invaluable; increasing strain upon the extant AVC arrangements during the fierce fighting at Mons and the Marne provoked the War Office to reconsider and asked the RSPCA to help them recruit more suitable men for the Corps, giving their blessing for them to set up an official fund to provide hospital equipment for sick and wounded horses. A further two hundred were soon recruited and trained by the RSPCA for the AVC. The first flag day was held in 1915, large panel adverts for the appeal regularly appeared in newspapers and magazines, and by the end of the war the fund had raised over £250,000. The money was well spent, providing a total of 180 horse ambulances,

'GOOD BYE, OLD MAN.'
Reproduced by permission of "The Sphere."

BLUE CROSS FUND.

Artist's impression, sold as a postcard, of a Blue Cross field dressing station for wounded horses.

Below: One of numerous RSPCA leaflets issued during the First World War.

Below left: A soldier and his mule, on one of many cold and misty days during the winter on the Western Front. (IWM Q1592)

twenty-six motor ambulances, tented field hospitals, a complete convalescent depot and thirteen hospitals in France with facilities for 13,500 horses and a host of horse comforts and veterinary necessities from woollen blankets, bandages and head collars to chaff cutters and corn crushers. Some 2,562,549 horses and mules were admitted to veterinary hospitals in France during the war.

The Anxious Need of Horses!—Taking up the Ammunition on the Western Front.

The Prime Minister said in his speech in the House of Commons, October 29th, that "two million horses had been transported across the seas to Allied Armies." It is to benefit some of these that

THE R.S.P.C.A. FUND NEEDS £50,000 AT ONCE

TO PROVIDE 5,000 MORE BEDS IN THE BRITISH HORSE HOSPITALS IN FRANCE

You love horses—you regret all the suffering of the horses in this War? Then you cannot refuse to help them. You cannot ignore this appeal to aid in providing the beds wherein they may rest comfortably while their wounds are tended, their hurts are healed.

The R.S.P.C.A. Fund is the only Fund authorised by the Army Council to assist the Army Veterinary Corps. Already, thanks to the generous British public, it has found over £120,000 in this good work. It now has to find another £50,000, to provide for 5,000 more horse beds costing, with necessary supplies, £10 each. It confidently awaits your help.

Our soldiers depend for their munitions, their food, their very lives on the horses. They recognize this in the sacrifice they make for the beloved horses. See overpage what the R.S.P.C.A. is doing for these horses, and share in this good and vital work.

The cost of this advertising is generously borne by a group of well-known sportsmen and horse-lovers. Your part is to send just whatever you can for the horses themselves.

CONTRIBUTION FORM.

Cut out this form, fill it in, and return with your Cheque or other remittance as promptly as possible to the Hon. Secretary, R.S.P.C.A. Fund, Dept. 00, 105, Jermyn Street, S.W.1.

I enclose £ .... towards the cost of the 5,000 extra beds (at £10 each) needed in the British Horse Hospitals in France.

Name ....

Address ....

Date ....

THE LORD GOD MADE THEM ALL

A NIMALS WORKING in the forces of all nations during the First World War came in all shapes and sizes, as did the many pets that soldiers found and adopted in trench, desert and prison camps. As we have seen, horses, mules and ponies all served with distinction in the desert but camels also provided a valuable mode of transport for General Allenby's campaign across the sands of the Middle East, notably across the Sinai Desert and during the Arab Revolt made so famous by T. E. Lawrence's accounts and the film epic based on them – *Lawrence of Arabia* (1962) – where bloody exchanges were fought between troops who had whipped their camels to charge. But predominantly, camels were used on campaign as they had been used for thousands of years – as beasts of burden. They carried everything from food and supplies to fantasses filled with precious drinking water, for troops fighting in a war in which victory depended on control and management of water supplies. The logistics of fighting a desert war using camels were staggering. For a start there was the equipment: most camels arrived with nothing more than a head collar, and British military authorities in the Middle East were given the task of obtaining 50,000 pack saddles. Then there was watering the beasts – a thirsty camel will drink 15–25 gallons of water – but if the camels were to stand in lakes or rivers they would soon develop foot problems. Watering places with troughs therefore had to be set up that were large enough to water a hundred camels at a time. These were no mean feat of construction: for example, at intervals along the valley of the Wadi Ghuzzeh more than 3,000 running feet of masonry and wooden troughs were provided for watering camels and horses.

Despite being known as 'the ships of the desert', camels were not always the graceful beasts of films; they could also be stubborn and cantankerous, no matter what the emergency, and did make a big target. They also suffered with numerous problems on campaign service: when food was served off the ground, as they licked it up they would gather in the grains of sand, which could cause colic and in turn fatal stomach ulcers; the saddles could cause sores; and mange was virulent – the labour involved in scraping the affected

Opposite:
More for a
souvenir than for
action, members
of the Norfolk
Yeomanry, like
many other
soldiers passing
through Egypt,
pose on camels
in front of
the Sphinx.

A touching study of a German Red Cross dog bringing succour to a wounded soldier.

Aufgespürt

parts and applying mange dressing to the bodies of tens of thousands of camels once a week meant the men of the Army Veterinary Corps involved in servicing the camels of the Middle East certainly had their work cut out. During the heavy fighting on the advance to Jerusalem in October, November and December 1917 the British lost 3,033 camels, of which 2,090 died of exposure, 601 were killed, 310 wounded, 29 missing and 3 were captured by the enemy.

The services performed by dogs during the First World War demonstrate loyalty, determination and courage again and again. Military training schools for dogs had been established in many countries including Sweden, Holland

I am DIK, and I belong to the Red Cross Service of the Belgian Army. I search for the wounded on the battlefields and I carry to them medicine and food in the pockets of my uniform, which is a white blanket with a red cross. I have been wounded myself. You will see my fore-paw is bandaged.

Will you buy the story of my life, written by Elizabeth Banks, with my portrait by Herbert Dicksee? It is called "Dik: A Dog of Belgium," and it costs one penny. It will tell you how I learned the difference between the Germans and the Belgians, and of something queer about my mother. The money you pay for my story and for this postcard helps the poor boys and girls of Belgium. The little Princess Marie José, our King's daughter, distributes it, and she also buys meal and biscuits for the Belgian War Dogs with the money you pay for my diamond-shape seal stamps. They are 3d. a dozen, and so are the postcards.

Although I live in Belgium, a London shop is very kindly lent to me by Canada's Grand Trunk Railway System, 19, Cockspur Street, S.W. Please call or write to me there, and don't forget to send me a stamp for reply.

DIK.

DÍK: A Dog of Belgium.

Advertising postcard for Dik, the dog of the Red Cross Service of the Belgian Army.

and Italy. The forces of France and Belgium had dog carts for supplies and ammunition; ironically, Germany had been buying suitable breeds of dogs from Britain and had 6,000 ready to serve when war broke out. Sentry dogs were used for their hearing and acute senses, especially in the hours of darkness while on patrol or on sentry duty in the field, to warn of the approach of the enemy. Few of these dogs gained any recognition, although one notable exception was a little ragged mongrel named Pyram, who was serving with the French Army and gave timely warning of the approach of enemy patrols, on many occasions foiling night attacks and undoubtedly saving many French lives. While President Poincare was visiting the front he took great interest in the canine warriors there and when he heard of the deeds of Pyram from his sergeant, the President asked an officer for a Scout Badge and fastened it to the dog's collar. By the latter part of the war, the French, Belgian and German forces had organised their own trained packs and driving dogs services which utilised the bigger, more powerful dogs at their disposal. Dogs were selected for the size, build and strength required for such tasks as delivering mail to the front and hauling supplies as varied as sand bags, barbed wire, ammunition and food.

A German messenger dog leaps a trench, near Sedan on the Western Front, May 1917. (IWM Q_050649)

Lieutenant Colonel
E. H. Richardson,
Commandant of
the British War
Dog Training
School.

Three dogs at
the Central Kennel
of the Messenger
Dog Service, GHQ.
Note that each
dog is wearing the
cylinder in which
the message was
to be carried.
(IWM Q 7345)

Dogs in the British Army, however, were a different matter. There was only one sentry dog in the British Army when war broke out, an Airedale attached to 1st Battalion, the Norfolk Regiment, when they proceeded to France in August 1914. The dog had been supplied by well-known dog trainer, Lieutenant Colonel E. H. Richardson. Richardson's proposals to set up a war dogs' training school were initially snubbed by the War Office but his offer to train ambulance dogs for the British Red Cross Society saw him proceed to Belgium with a few dogs in August 1914. Ambulance dogs could be found in many of the belligerent armies during the war, as their keen sense of smell and hearing could be trained to seek out casualties upon the battlefield even if they were buried or hidden by debris.

Richardson's work was both worthy and worthwhile: while he was over in France he answered a number of requests for sentry dogs with more of his favoured Airedales. During the winter of 1916 Richardson received a request from a Royal Artillery officer for trained dogs to run communications between his outpost and the battery. After a number of trials with various dogs Richardson found two Airedales, named Wolf and Prince, who would carry messages homewards regularly over 2 miles. Deployed into active service their work was soon recognised and wheels were at last set in motion for the establishment of a training school for messenger dogs. This was formed a few months later at Shoeburyness in Essex, because the big guns of the artillery that were fired in training nearby would also provide excellent training for the dogs to get used to regular gunfire. The school was a success and soon moved to Lyndhurst in the New Forest, Hampshire.

The men who staffed the unit were drawn from those men who had previously been gamekeepers, hunt servants and shepherds. The dogs themselves were initially chosen from dogs' homes at Battersea, Birmingham, Bristol and Manchester; then appeals were sent to constabularies all over the country for stray dogs of certain breeds; finally the War Office appealed to the public to send their dogs as gifts. When sending a loved domestic pet many people wrote moving letters to accompany them. One woman wrote, 'I have given my husband and my sons, and now he too is required, I give my dog.' Each new dog recruit was carefully tested for aptitude for three special duties – messenger, sentry or guard dog. Most found their niche and entered into the work like a new game. The dogs that proved best suited were

Signals armband as worn by members of the Royal Engineers messenger service.

Cap badge of the Royal Engineers.

A member of the Royal Engineers (Signals) puts a message into the cylinder attached to the collar of a messenger dog, Étaples, August 1918. (IWM Q_009276)

sheepdogs, lurchers and Airedales; any dog who showed no desire for work was sent back to where it had come from.

The trained dogs were sent to a number of theatres of war, notably the Balkans and the Western Front, where camps with long lines of kennels stretched out – like tiny soldiers' huts in a model army camp – and Richardson kept all the reports he received of the gallant work of the dogs he had trained. A number of them were published in his book *British War Dogs*, among them this letter from Private Osbourne, the keeper of Jim, a retriever-spaniel cross, who had reliably covered distances of up to 4½ miles with a speed estimated to be in excess of three or four times that of a soldier runner:

You will be gratified to learn that little 'Jim' by his excellent services and consistency has justly earned our CO's commendation who thinks he is easily the finest dog in France... Jim was instrumental in first giving the warning of gas, due no doubt to his highly sensitive nose, thereupon he was immediately released with the warning to Headquarters, arriving there a little more than three-quarters of an hour earlier than the warning given by wire. His worth is beyond value and his services beyond praise and I feel honoured to take care of such a very serviceable animal.

There were not only trained dogs on the front lines: many senior officers took their faithful gun dog with them. Indeed, it was rare to find a military airfield without a dog in Britain, France and Flanders, and the most

notorious of the German aces, Manfred von Richtoven ('The Red Baron') adored his pet dog Moritz. One of the most famous of the officers' pets was General Charles Townsend's fox terrier Spot, who was with his master during the siege of Kut al Mara during the Mesopotamia campaign and obtained the *nom de guerre* of 'Spot o' Kut'. When the besieged garrison finally fell in April 1916 Townsend was taken to Constantinople and wanted his dog with him, but this was against regulations, so Spot was sent down the Tigris with a special escort under the flag of truce and delivered to the British forces that had been sent to relieve Kut, and was returned to England. Another famous dog was Jack, the pet dog of nurse Edith Cavell. Cavell was executed by German firing squad in occupied Belgium in October 1915 having been found guilty of 'conducting soldiers to the enemy'. It was difficult to find a new home for Jack after his mistress's execution as people feared being branded sympathisers if they took him on. Ill from neglect and worry, Jack was eventually taken on by the Dowager Duchess of Croy, who nursed him back to health; he lived on into the 1920s.

America's first war dog was Boston Bull terrier Sergeant Stubby, who had been found wandering in the grounds of Yale Field, New Haven Connecticut where soldiers were in training. Stubby soon became well liked by the men and he was despatched to the trenches of France, serving with 102nd, 26th (Yankee) Division, where he was present at four offensives and seventeen battles. Proving himself invaluable for giving advance warning of gas attacks and finding wounded soldiers among the debris of the battlefield, he was eventually removed from the line after he was wounded by grenade fragments. Stubby recovered, was heralded a war hero and his story was told in newspapers across the states – receiving awards from both France and America, Sergeant Stubby became the most decorated dog of the First World War.

Of all the animal stories of the First World War one of the most remarkable is that of Prince, the Irish terrier owned by Private Brown of

Sergeant Stubby, the most decorated dog of the First World War, basking in the glories of retirement in 1921.

the 1st Battalion, North Staffordshire Regiment. Brown left his home in Hammersmith and proceeded with his battalion to France and Flanders in August 1914. In late September his wife was alarmed to find that Prince was missing; she heard nothing of him until some weeks later, when she received news in a letter from her husband in France that the dog was with him! He had been brought to Private Brown from the front-line trenches, and the only possible explanation for this remarkable feat was that Prince must have got in with some troops, crossed over with them and by some small wonder found his master.

Private Brown of the 1st Battalion, North Staffordshire Regiment, with his dog Prince, who found his way from his home in England and was reunited with his master near the front line in France.

THE LORD GOD MADE THEM ALL

Carrier pigeons feature in the story of the First World War from its outbreak, during the August and September spy scares of 1914 when Britain was rife with fears of invasion and enemy agents. Precautions against correspondence with Germany by the police and post office meant that the only way of communicating with Germany (or so it was believed at the time) was via pigeon post. The initial response was for all pigeons along the coast to be interned at police stations or destroyed. The possession of homing pigeons was only allowed with a permit and railway companies banned the transport of carrier pigeons. This was no joke: the law was swift to act and in a number of cases naturalised Germans or people of German descent living in Britain were hauled before the

NORFOLK CONSTABULARY

NOTICE!

SHOOTING HOMING PIGEONS

Killing, Wounding or Molesting Carrier or Homing Pigeons
is punishable under the Defence of the Realm Regulations by

SIX MONTHS' IMPRISONMENT OR £100 FINE.

The public are reminded that Carrier and Homing Pigeons are doing valuable work for the Government, and are requested to assist in the suppression of the shooting of these birds.

A REWARD of £5

will be paid by the General Officer Commanding Northern Army, Home Defence, for information securing conviction for killing or concealing Naval or Military Carrier Pigeons.

Information should be given to the Police or nearest Military Post or to the General Officer Commanding Northern Army, H. D., Norwich.

Any person who finds a Carrier or Homing Pigeon dead or incapable of flight and who neglects forthwith to hand it over or send it to some military post or police constable in the neighbourhood with information as to the place where the pigeon was found; or, having obtained information as to any Carrier or Homing Pigeon being killed or found incapable for flight, neglects forthwith to communicate the information to a military post or to a police constable in the neighbourhood is liable, on conviction, to the punishment above described.

J. H. MANDER, *Captain,*

County Police Station,   Chief Constable.
     Castle Meadow, Norwich,
November 1917.

Roberts & Co., Printers, Ten Bell Lane, Norwich.

police courts and faced stiff penalties for owning homing pigeons. Anton Lambert, a German living in Plaistow, was sentenced at West Ham Police Court in September 1914 to six months' hard labour for having twenty-four homing pigeons in his possession. It also became an offence under the Defence of the Realm Regulations to shoot, kill, wound or molest homing pigeons. Culprits could face up to six months' imprisonment or a £100 fine.

A warning of the stiff penalties for those who would shoot or molest homing pigeons in wartime.

The valuable work of the Emergency Pigeon Service was established when private owners supplied pigeons to minesweepers, who were then enabled to send information on newly laid minefields and other dangers via our feathered friends – many a patrol boat owed its continued existence to pigeons. French troops were already using pigeons on the Western Front when the first British Pigeon Service was raised and the first sixty men enlisted into it in July 1915. The first British pigeons were sent over to France in March 1916 and similar services were soon developed in Salonika, Egypt and Mesopotamia.

It is a little-known fact that tanks also carried pigeons; with no radios the pigeon provided their only effective means of communication and were

Pigeon Service message and leg ring with canister. (IWM COM 1102)

Canadian soldiers release a carrier pigeon from a trench on the Western Front. (IWM CO 1414)

key to the success of a number of actions. For example, during the battle for Arras two tanks with pigeons on board saw large bodies of German troops massing behind the hills. They were about 22 miles (35 kilometres) from the base, but within forty minutes the British Artillery had received the message via the pigeons. British heavy artillery were brought to bear and a dangerous counter-attack was smashed.

What became known as the 'Carrier Service' was led by respected pre-war pigeon fancier Lieutenant Colonel A. H. Osman and was run almost entirely by volunteers. Pigeons were often bred by British men of the working class; in 1916 alone, 20,000 pigeons worth £20,000–£30,000 were acquired, bred and supplied by fanciers who owned the best pedigree stock. Osman was backed up by a special staff of expert officers who worked with fanciers and every pigeon loft on every front was manned by enlisted soldiers who had been experienced pigeon racers in civilian life.

A pigeon being released from a porthole in the side of a tank, near Albert, France. (IWM Q 9247)

Releasing a pigeon to call for rescue from a Royal Naval Air Service float plane, 1917.

The Royal Flying Corps, Royal Air Force and Royal Naval Air Service were also grateful to pigeons, for they carried them on their aircraft, particularly those who had over-sea-patrol flying duties. One poignant story is that of pigeon no. NURP/17/F.16331. On 5 September 1917 Squadron Commander Vincent Nicholl was flying a DH4 aircraft with Flight Lieutenant Trewin from RNAS Great Yarmouth on an anti-Zeppelin patrol when its engine seized and the aircraft came down in a rough North Sea and soon sank. Bob Leckie was piloting flying boat 866, spotted their predicament, went to their rescue and his crew managed to haul the two nearly drowned men out of the water. There were now six men on the flying boat and all Leckie's attempts to get it off the sea failed. Faced with the task of taxiing back in an overloaded boat with a heavy following sea, they launched a total of four pigeons carrying messages of their location and situation. Eventually both engines ran out of petrol; the situation was desperate and the men were very ill with sea-sickness but they just had to keep bailing out the plane as otherwise it would have sunk. At 11.30 am on 8 September the message

Nicholl had sent three days earlier was delivered at the air station. Pigeon NURP/17/F.16331 had been found dead with exhaustion on a beach a few miles away by locally based soldiers; the bird and the message were taken to the War Signalling station and the message was telephoned through. The search that had been abandoned with all hope lost was resumed. All six crew were rescued in the nick of time. The gallant pigeon was stuffed and displayed in a case in the mess; on the case was fixed a brass plaque bearing the inscription, 'A very gallant gentleman.'

Soldiers have always acquired pets when on campaign service – often these were small animals, easy to hide away in a pack or a pocket – and many had a practical use. Just as on ships, cats were a welcome addition in rat-infested billets and dugouts, as were feisty terriers keen on ratting; these animals did much to keep down the rodent population in the trenches. Pets were not only valued for practical reasons: soldiers are human beings

The 'Very Gallant Gentleman', a pigeon who saved the lives of six Royal Naval Air Services airmen but lost his own life in the process.

and among the degradation, death and inhumanity the innocent play and affection of a kitten or puppy transcend the darkness. Many soldiers carried their pets with them wherever they went, even into action, and saw them as their lucky mascot or talisman, such as 22-year-old Londoner, Private Alfred Dyson Freeman of the 1st Battalion, Honourable Artillery Company, who was killed in action in the trenches near Mailley-Mallet in October 1916. The battalion war diary records, 'His kitten which he carried as a mascot was asleep on his chest when he was found.'

In the theatres of war around the world all manner of animals were adopted by solders: in India, where there are many dangerous snakes, a mongoose was a popular and useful pet; in the deserts of Palestine many soldiers adopted friendly little jerboas, a number of which were found under helmets, in pockets and packs after the battle. Prisoners of war were often allowed to keep animals – it certainly helped to relieve boredom and frustration while in incarceration. Some were allowed dogs or cats while others tamed mice or birds.

Even on the home front pet animals did their bit too: a number of accounts survive of dogs who were known to be keen of hearing and would yelp and bark in an unusual way when they heard Zeppelin engines and became valuable for giving early warning of the approaching raiders. It was also found that pheasants became unsettled and vocal when they heard such engines and a number of pheasant coops were placed at key positions along the east coast of England as another means of alerting authorities of the approach of Zeppelins.

Opposite: Officers of the Machine Gun Corps and one Portuguese Captain (front right) with some little friends they found along the way in France.

Tommies and their pets – a superb cover from The War Illustrated, *June 1917.*

Jim, the coastguard Airedale who gave warnings of approaching Zeppelins. (IWM Q 24145)

A Tommy's little jerboa pet, 'the desert rat', made so famous by Eighth Army in the Second World War, perched on the inside lining of his helmet, Palestine 1917.

LEGACIES

THE LEGACIES of the First World War are still felt today. The work of the RSPCA and Our Dumb Friends League brought humane care and comfort to animals both at home and abroad during the war; their work continues to this day – in fact ODFL is now known by its old name as The Blue Cross, and the Royal Army Veterinary Corps provides some of the finest veterinary care in the world for military horses, dogs and mascots. Above all we should not forget the debt of gratitude we owe to those loyal animals who did so much in the First World War. They had no choice, but they gave their all in the greatest war the world had ever seen.

Party of British troops resting by a wrecked building in Athies during the German retreat to the Hindenburg Line, April 1917. (IWM Q1978)

Thousands of ex-military horses were returned home from the Western Front and sold off over the ensuing months at auctions around the country. Many of them went out to work on farms or pull a delivery cart and spent the rest of their lives in peace. The Editor of *John Bull* magazine suggested to ODFL that an 'Order of Merit' badge should be issued and attached to the tack of all ex-military horses. Shaped in a heart with a Blue Cross in the centre it bore the legend 'Treat Me Well – I have done my bit.' It was intended that the badge would serve as a reminder to their owners and drivers to treat them well in view of the services they had rendered to their country.

Tragically the Armistice did not end well for all of them. In many cases the dog or horse that had served his country loyally, rather than being returned home, was destroyed instead. Perhaps worse than destruction was the treatment of 20,000 military horses in Palestine. Too expensive to bring home, they were repaid for their services by being cast (discharged from military service) and sold in Egypt to be cruelly mistreated or worked to death in quarries. There was an initial outcry about these horses – some soldiers found out the fate that awaited their mounts and at the last moment took them out into the desert and shot their dear old horse. The tragic memory of having to despatch their loyal mount remained vivid in the minds of many of the

The Animals in War Memorial, Brook Gate, Park Lane, London, opened by HRH the Princess Royal on 24 November 2004.

troopers into old age. Thank goodness for Mrs Dorothy Brooke, who rescued 3,072 horses and mules in Egypt between 1932 and 1934, and a further 4,000 in Belgium through ODFL – raising and spending £40,000 for the operation.

In a nation of animal lovers, where stones, crosses and plaques mark the graves of long-passed regimental mascots, there was no single memorial to animals that had 'done their bit' in war. Only after the publication of Jilly Cooper's moving book *Animals in War* was a campaign begun, with Jilly as a co-trustee and great campaigner for the cause. A fund of £1.4 million was raised for the creation of the remarkable Portland stone memorial with bronze animal figures of a horse, dog and mules laden with kit, designed by sculptor David Backhouse. The Animals in War memorial was opened by Princess Anne in November 2004.

The main inscription on the memorial states:

> This monument is dedicated to all the animals that served and died alongside
> British and allied forces in wars and campaigns throughout time.

It concludes with the poignant words, 'They had no choice.'

FURTHER READING

Baker, P. S. *Animal War Heroes*. A & C Black, 1933.

Baynes, E. H. *Animal Heroes of the Great War*. Macmillan, 1925.

Blenkinsop, Major-General Sir L. J. and Rainey, Lt. Col. J. W. (eds.) *Official History of the War Veterinary Service*. HMSO, 1925.

Brereton, J. M. *The Horse in War*. David & Charles, 1976.

Butler, S. *Goodbye Old Friend*. Halsgrove, 2012.

Butler, S. *The War Horses*. Halsgrove, 2011.

Charrington, Major H. V. S. *The 12th Royal Lancers in France 1914–1918*. Gale & Polden, 1921.

Cooper, J. *Animals at War*. Corgi, 2000.

Edwards, Major T. J. *Mascots and Pets of the Services*. Gale & Polden, 1953.

Galtrey, Captain S. *The Horse and the War*. Country Life, 1918.

Gardiner, J. *The Animals' War*. Portrait, 2006.

Gladstone, H. *Birds and the War*. Skeffington, 1919.

Gray, E. A. *Dogs of War*. Robert Hale, 1989.

Hall, Major R. J. G. *The Australian Light Horse*. W. D. Joynt, 1968.

Hamer, B. *Dogs at War: True Stories of Canine Courage Under Fire*. Carlton, 2001.

Harfield, A. *Pigeon to Packhorse: The Illustrated Story of Animals in Army Communications*. Picton Publishing, 1989.

Hogue, O. *The Cameliers*. Andrew Melrose, 1919.

Inchbald, G. *Camels and Others*. Johnson, 1968.

Inchbald, G. *With the Imperial Camel Corps*. Johnson, 1968.

Kramer, J. J. *Animal Heroes: Military Mascots and Pets*. Secker & Warburg, 1982.

Le Chêne, E. *Silent Heroes: The Bravery and Devotion of Animals in War*. Souvenir Press, 1994.

Lemish, M. G. *War Dogs: The First Comprehensive History of the Military Dog*. Brasseys, 1996.

McCafferty, G. *They Had No Choice: Racing Pigeons at War*. Tempus, 2000.

Moss, A. W. *Valiant Crusade: The History of the Royal Society for the Prevention of Cruelty to Animals*. Cassell, 1961.

Osman, Lt. Col. A. H. *Pigeons in the Great War*. Racing Pigeon Publishing Co. (n.d.).

Richardson, Lt. Col. E. H. *British War Dogs*. Skeffington, 1920.

Smith, C. *The Blue Cross at War*. Blue Cross, 1990.

Tamblyn, Lt. Col. D. S. *The Horse in War*. Country Life, 1918.

Van Emden, R. *Tommy's Ark*. Bloomsbury, 2010.

Walker, G. Goold. *The Honourable Artillery Company in the Great War 1914–1919*. Seeley, Service & Co., 1930.

TRAINING MANUALS

Animal Management. HMSO, London, 1908 (reprinted 1914).

Cavalry Training. HMSO, London 1912 (reprinted with amendments 1915).

PLACES TO VISIT

Imperial War Museum London, Lambeth Road SE1 6HZ.
Telephone: 020 7416 5000. Website: www.iwm.org.uk

National Army Museum, Royal Hospital Road, Chelsea, London SW3 4HT.
Telephone: 020 7881 6606. Website: www.nam.ac.uk

National Maritime Museum, Park Row, Greenwich, London SE10 9NE.
Telephone: 020 8858 4422. Website: www.rmg.co.uk

'Firepower': Royal Regiment of Artillery Museum, The Royal Arsenal, Woolwich,
London SE18 6ST. Telephone: 020 8855 7755.
Website: www.firepower.org.uk

Members of the 12th Lancers at Thorpe railway station, Norwich, in 1914, lances leaning against the wall, ready to load their horses onto the cattle wagons to begin their journey to France with the British Expeditionary Force.

INDEX